COACHING KIDS

All TEAM SPORTS

Published by Price World Publishing, LLC
1300 W. Belmont Ave, Suite 20G
Chicago, IL 60657

Cover Design by Dianne T. Goh
Book layout by Raja Sekar R
Illustrations by Howard Venezia
Editing by Lisa Reuter
Proofreading by Jenn Sodini
Printing by Sheridan Books

Second Edition, February 2011
ISBN: 978-1-932549-62-1
Library of Congress Control Number: 2010920934

Printed in the United States of America

10 9 8 7 6 5 4 3 2 1

COACHING KIDS

All TEAM SPORTS

2nd Editon

by
Frank (Duke) Watts

Inspiration for this book comes primarily from the kids and parents who so graciously put up with my blunders as I learned to coach. My thanks must also include my own kids, Jenna, Robert and Bill, and my wife, Jane, who likewise suffered. May my grandchildren Zeb, Avery, Cassie, Abby, Gabby, and Jackson not suffer as much and perhaps even prosper from this work.

Contents

Foreword	06
Introduction	09
Sports, Love, and Lament	15
Competition	21
Paid Coaches or Volunteer Parents?	24
Can You Coach Kids?	31
Clear and Simple – Assume Nothing	36
Behavior	46
The Organized Coach	50
Involve the Parents	58

Parent-Player Meeting 68

Win at All Costs? 76

Protect the Kids and Yourself 81

Intensity 85

Problem Parents 95

The League 101

Purge the Troublemakers 107

Balance the Playing Time 113

Balance the Talent 119

Dropouts 125

Competitive or Noncompetitive 129

Plan and Communicate 133

Coaches' Training 137

Schools and Kids Sports 141

Recreation Districts and Kids Sports 148

Rewards and Beginning 152

Foreword

What ever happened to playing ball in the front yard? Pick-up games at the park? When we were kids, we'd come home from school, grab a snack, and head outside to play. Everyone in the neighborhood would gather in the street, choose sides, and start playing in our favorite sport, whichever one was in-season.

We created games using the equipment we had. We played every position and called our own plays. Often times we'd play until mom called us for dinner by flashing the porch light a few hundred times.

Things are different now that technology has changed the world. Kids play video games instead of riding their bikes. They text and tweet instead of playing Nerf hoops in the garage. Man, we had some killer Nerf hoops tournaments back in the day.

Now we parents have to schedule everything. With schools cutting physical education and sports programs, club sports have become increasingly popular, thus increasing the need for volunteer coaches and parental involvement.

I know this because I've seen it from all angles. I've coached, directed, and administered basketball teams, camps, clinics, and tournaments for over 25 years. I've coached boys and girls, men and women. I've coached my two sons' teams (flag football, Pop Warner football, t-ball, basketball) since they were three years old.

I was fortunate enough to be the head coach of an NCAA Division I women's basketball program at Santa Clara University that played in the NCAA Tournament, which was broadcast on ESPN no less. I was head coach and president of operations of a men's minor league professional team, which basically meant that besides coaching I had to sweep the gym, sell the tickets, and call time-outs. Today I run my own company called NetScouts Basketball.

Between my time as an NCAA coach and today, I had the pleasure of working as the coach and director of a basketball club in London, England. In London, we had young men, women, and kids from over 20 different countries on our teams, along with the one thing that brought them all together – basketball

The differences in youth-sports culture were illuminating. It has always been very important for me as the coach to have some help coordinating all of the various responsibilities that go along with running one team, not to mention four. Parents in the UK aren't accustomed to driving kids to games, or even to attending the games for that matter. Snacks? Forget about it. Kids hop on those cool red buses or ride the subway to and from games by themselves. It's amazing that there are no "soccer moms" in London! I needed help, so I had to change all that –I had to get the parents involved.

By the time my family and I left London, my organization had changed. It now had great parental involvement, with record numbers of kids joining. The parents were really enjoying being a part of something as well. Also, after parental involvement improved, my job became a little less hectic, which allowed me to coach their kids and teach them the game.

If you're reading this, you're probably thinking about coaching your son or daughter's little league team. Or even better, you already decided to coach and you're wondering to yourself "what do I do now"?

Well, lucky for you Duke Watts came along and wrote this book. I will answer most, if not all, of your questions and give you the tools to be successful as a youth level coach.

On my most recent basketball business trip to Europe, I saw two things that made me smile. The first was a pick-up game of basketball in a park in Madrid. These kids were playing three-on-two, using a soccer ball that didn't bounce very well, and loving every minute of it. The other inspiring thing I saw was a two-versus-two game of soccer at a bus stop. The kids were using an aluminum can as 'la pelota' (the ball). It made me think of our own ad-hoc games on the sandlot. Those were the days.

-Chris Denker, Managing Partner of NetScouts Basketball LLC, "The International Basketball Connection"™

Introduction

Have you ever:

- Heard an angry coach hollering at his kids to "play ball" and wondered what that meant?
- Coached a kids team against the league organizer, who "just happened" to have more talented kids on his team?
- Heard a parent lament that "sports shouldn't be so competitive"?
- Been asked by the Recreation District to sign a pledge to "stay out of the process"?
- Seen bottom performers forced off their team?
- Witnessed a parent hollering obscenities at a coach or official?
- Witnessed a coach who allowed his players to swear on the field?
- Seen the parents malign the coac
- Heard the coach malign the parents?

- Witnessed a coach who obviously didn't want the parents to "interfere"?

These typical problems make it sound like we have some bad people involved in coaching. By my experience, it usually isn't the people – it's the process.

Much has been written about coaching kids. Most books are sport-specific, covering only one sport. They go into considerable depth on that sport. Certainly, if you're going to coach any sport, you should find and read a book on that sport that is applicable to young kids.

Some other books are general, mostly feel-good stuff. They often focus on how to make the participants feel better, not necessarily perform better. This refers to sports with no winners or losers – as if there is some sport that exists in which there are no winners or losers! You will find little written, however, that relates directly to the basic challenge of coaching kids of young ages, regardless of the sport. You'll find even less on organizing kids sports from the coach and league viewpoints.

I will draw heavily on my own experience playing sports, coaching, and watching many other coaches to make my points. Many, many discussions with other youth coaches have allowed me to develop some principles about team-sport coaching and organizing, whether it's baseball, basketball, field hockey, football, flag football, ice hockey, lacrosse, rugby, soccer, softball, tee ball, track, volleyball, or any other team sports I have not mentioned. I will also inject a little humor – as little as you will find anywhere!

This book will address coaching and organizing kindergarten through middle school, covering the coaching basics that are applicable to any team sport. Coaching high school kids is generally a different issue, for better or worse. Somewhere in the late middle-school years, the principles begin to change toward the exclusion of parents. This book, however, will not explore whether or not this should be the case. We will stick with the younger years because that is where my experience is.

This book is about coaching kids at a very impressionable stage of life – a stage when they will learn to love the sport or not, play it well or not, appreciate competition or not, become a fan or not, or progress to the next level or not. Coaches must be aware of this and do everything in their power to help kids both appreciate the sport and progress as rapidly as possible. Some of what is found here may be worthwhile life lessons.

I will also look closely at the league organization and its duties. This is an often-ignored aspect of kids sports. I'm very dogmatic about what should or should not be done. Keep in mind that there are exceptions to all rules. Writing about the possible exceptions would make this work longer and dilute the message. Thus, only a little time will be spent writing about exceptions.

Also remember that my rules are based on mistakes I have made. They man not necessarily be the best approach. You may be wondering just what qualifies me, a mistake-making, ordinary coach to write about coaching kids.

Like many others, I played many summer and winter sports in the "sandlots." I played many different organized sports, earned a few high school letters, shared in the raising of three kids, coached several different team sports for 26 kid-seasons, taught skiing to disabled kids for five seasons, discussed coaching at some length with other coaches, and observed many paid and volunteer coaches at work. I have loved almost every minute of it. I also have been totally disorganized and watched other coaches in the same fix. I found my way out of the disorganization by trial and error. Hopefully you will not have to go through as much of this as I did.

As mentioned before, I know most of the team sports well, but I'm not qualified to tell you how to coach. This coach is only able to tell you how to avoid mistakes when coaching kids, because I have done just about as well as the worst. I have arguably made more mistakes than any other volunteer coach in modern history. You can certainly do better.

Chapter 1

Sports, Love, and Lament

Kids' sports represent what's best about America. Sports offer a chance for the player to get fit while having fun. Sports offer fun for participants and their families, establish a set of rules, reward those for most who participate the most, and usually provide consequences for those who break the rules.

Sports offer the excitement of competition as an individual and with a team. They offer an opportunity to excel. They offer an opportunity to belong. Team sports teach kids practical lessons in teamwork. Kids learn how to win and learn how to act after they win or lose. Also, they learn how to lead, follow, or get out of the way.

Sports offer a cleansing of the mind from school, work, or family pressures. There is typically a clear outcome with little fuzziness. There is a kinship found in sports that is lacking in many other endeavors. Many characteristics of sports are often and should always be prevalent in other life pursuits.

A good teacher of any team sport puts heavy emphasis on the mental aspects of the game. Wasn't it Yogi Berra who said, "Ninety percent of this game is half mental"? Even at young ages, the mental aspect of the game needs to be part of the training. It also needs to be part of the coach's preparation and execution.

Yes, sports have a dark side. Some college and professional athletes are the worst role models. Some end up in jail or dead. The news media folks have a fixation about reporting such events.

They seldom put them in perspective, however. What percentage of our pro or college athletes do such things? Even in the pro ranks, where money can corrupt, the percentage is very small. But that isn't the impression you get from the news. Unfortunately, this is the image some parents have. You and I can't do much about the news media except complain. The same is true with umpires. But we can show kids a good role model and teach them what teamwork means.

As Terry Frei wrote in *Third Down and a War to Go*, "Done right, sports teach. Sports bond. Sports enrich. Sports are about lessons and unbreakable friendships that can last through one man's lifetime. And longer."

At dinner the other evening, a friend commented that the sandlots are empty. Where did the kids go? How often do you see kids playing in an empty lot, field, or greenbelt these days, with the kids themselves organizing the contest as they choose, playing a game without adults, and learning how to get along with their peers? Are all the kids at home watching TV?

When we were young, we often just chose sides and played without coaches, officials, or direct supervision. Did it hurt our self-esteem to be chosen last? Sure, but we got over it, and that taught us one of life's hard lessons: We are all good and bad at something, and finding our strengths and weaknesses is part of life.

On the local ball field, we seldom had enough players to make two baseball teams, so "piggy-move-up" was the option of choice. In elementary school, a couple of teachers were usually on the playground, but they were just there to settle arguments. That is, if they could get to us before a fight broke out. Yes, we had fights on occasion. It didn't seem to hurt us. It was good preparation for the boxing team. Probably those fights worked off some of the frustration that today might lead to some kid bringing a gun or knife to school.

We usually learned how to settle our problems without fighting. I especially remember the tackle football games in grade school. Yes, we had tackle football in grade school – without pads or helmets! Can you imagine that happening in a modern school? We spent hours and hours on a field, on the ice, and at the backyard hoop all with no supervision. We traded, negotiated, bartered, blackmailed, and threatened to take the ball or puck and go home. But we played, talked "smack," and, most of all, had fun.

Our typical mode of operation was to have the two best players choose teams. The guy who chose first had to face uphill. The guy who chose last had to face downhill. Playing slightly downhill had an obvious advantage. Kids have a way of "leveling the playing field."

Perhaps we should still let kids do their own thing like we once did. But today, most parent(s) are working, and no one is home to keep one eye on the sandlot. So, for better or worse, adults have organized sports, structured them, and turned them into a highly programmed activity. Now we need to figure out how to make kids sports the best possible experience for all involved.

Nothing like a
Solid connection.

Chapter 2

Competition

We were competitive. Most of us wanted to win no matter what the game. There was nothing wrong with competition. Today is no different in that regard. Boys are especially naturally competitive. Though, as girls' sports have emerged they have also become very competitive. But I digress.

Should youth sports be competitive? Yes. But do they need to be so adult-driven? At what age should kids be organized and coached by adults? Can we return to the sandlot? Maybe we can if one parent is home when the kids aren't in school and knows where the kids are at all times. Maybe we will as soon as outhouses make a comeback! So what should we do? The best scenario is to develop an association of volunteer parents to organize, coach, and assist the coach. Or, in a school or recreation district, we should take an approach that involves the parents in a meaningful fashion.

Can we combine the best of the sandlot with organized youth sports? Can or should a competitive sport culture be kept out of organized youth sports? Should there be a clear separation of competitive and noncompetitive leagues? Can we combine the best of the sandlot, organization, and competition? Should the noncompetitive league just not keep score? Will the kids, parents, and coaches on both sides feel like winners?

This book won't answer all these questions, but it will make you think about what is best for the kids and not what is best for the parents, the teachers, the city, the recreation district, the coaches, the administrators, or the school board. I emphasize again that this book is about doing what is best for the kids.

Chapter 3

Paid Coaches or Volunteer Parents?

Who should coach kids? The short answer is: anyone who is interested in helping a kid learn how to play a sport and have fun at it. To be considered an effective coach by the kids and parents, however, is still another challenge.

Since the early days of sandlots, kid-coaching has been a challenge equal to finding a needle in a haystack. Because of this, some folks think professional coaches should be hired to coach kids. They say that kids sports should be left up to the recreation district (meaning government), to hire the coaches. Some people think they need someone with a recreation degree, a "real pro" who knows what he is doing. These people often think that parents should take a pledge to stay out of the process. This is the modern trend. Other folks think parents should organize and coach kid sports. I favor parents doing the organizing and coaching at young ages for reasons that will become apparent. You can decide for yourself.

The coach may be a parent, teacher, or recreation district professional. Whether done by paid or volunteer coaches, however, the parents must not be left out of the process. Parents often know the sport as well as anyone. They know kids better. They have a vested interest in both the process and the outcome. There is nothing taught in college that trumps parents' knowledge of their kids.

Yes, sometimes parents are destructive. Sometimes they get carried away – too far away. This is often a problem with the process, not the parent.

On occasion, problem parents do need to be purged from the organization. When the government is in control, it's very difficult to purge troublemakers. How can the government tell a taxpayer to take a hike? It can't, and it doesn't. Thus, the school or recreation district asks all parents to take a pledge to stay out of the process. Yes, the rare parent is a troublemaker. But parents come at no cost. No taxes are needed to pay parent coaches. For all these reasons, parental organizing and coaching of kids' team sports is generally better than using professionals.

Paid coaches generally think they have to do it all alone. After all, isn't that what they are paid for? Therefore, they exclude the parents. Sometimes, recreation districts adopt the paid coach approach. They typically ask parents to sign a pledge to "keep out of it." This is exactly the wrong approach!

The paid coach will want a paid assistant, paid mileage, trips for training, seminars for improvement, and other costly extras ad nauseam. Then the organization needs more money to throw at "the problems." Often, these very problems are created by excluding parents.

Don't believe the mantra that "parents are different now than in the past." They "don't want to be involved" or "don't have time to be involved." Parents are no different now than they ever were. Their kids are usually number one in their hearts and minds. They want to see their kids get the best teaching and training available. They want to see them succeed. They generally want to be involved in their kids' sports. They will find the time to be involved. In kids' sports, there are many ancillary jobs that don't take much time but will get the parents involved, as I will discuss later.

Who needs the government to coach kids' sports anyway? Probably those parents who want someone to baby-sit their kid. Should we pay taxes to make youth sports a baby-sitting service? The few parents who don't want to be involved should hire a baby sitter, not dump their kids on a coach. An association of parents, with parents coaching and helping, is the better choice.

Volunteer parents should be used to coach, officiate, organize, and administrate. Parents should coach the kids and organize the program while the government should furnish the field, rink, park, or court and pledge to stay out of the process. The parents lead, the kids follow, and the government gets out of the way.

Having said this, I recognize that paid coaches may be here to stay in some communities. Whether they work for a recreation districts or schools, paid coaches should still include the parents in the process. Paid coaches and their organizations should follow the rules I'm recommending.

Whether you are a volunteer or paid, realize that some days nothing works. That is how it will seem. That's the time to put the mind to work over the matter. If nothing seems to be working, it is probably for lack of positive planning, thinking, training, and practice – coach's responsibilities. Think over what went wrong and resolve to correct it by the next practice.

Some days—
Nothing works!

Chapter 4

Can You Coach Kids?

So you think you can coach kids. You know you can. After all, you have played the game – perhaps even excelled at the game. You know the rules. You have studied the fine points, watched the pros, and understand the strategy. All of this qualifies you to be a semi-failure when coaching kids. Lots of kid-coaches have those qualifications. Lots of us have been partial failures in our first season or two. For example, knowing your sport too well may cause you to make your teaching too complex for young kids.

I'm talking here about the formative years of elementary and middle school. When we are with young kids we need to keep it simple. Basics. More Basics. Add slight nuances depending upon the age.

In fact, if you're a real student of the sport and it's your hobby, then your chances of failure with young kids may be greater than the next coach's. You will probably lose them before your first practice is over, instead of somewhere around the third game as I did. Of course, younger kids need more simplification than older middle school players.

I'll use baseball as an example. At earlier ages, with someone on first and a ground ball hit to the infield, forget the double play. Keep it simple. Teach your players to make the throw to first and get the easy out. As they get older, teach them to cut down the lead runner. Then, at a later age, go for the double play. At exactly what age depends on the talent available.

Now don't burn this book and call the league to tell them to forget it. You can coach. You will do a much better job than I did. You will also probably learn more than the kids will. And it will likely be more rewarding for you than for the kids.

The coach's first priority must be to help young players enjoy the game. If they are having fun and practice moves fast, they will learn easily. If instructions or expectations are too complex, it will be difficult for both you and them to have fun.

I want you to have just enough doubt about your kid-coaching ability to finish this book. Maybe you can learn from this coach's 472 mistakes. I'm well-qualified to tell you how to make mistakes when coaching kids. Please do not panic. I will not cover all 472 mistakes. I can't even remember them all. I have, however, made some (or seen some made) over and over, and I remember those well. I will frequently slip into my coach's ego and tell you how to do it "right."

Experience is the best teacher, so don't expect to progress without mistakes. Just resolve to recognize them and correct them as soon as is practical, which will probably be in the next practice instead of in a game. This book may help you avoid some mistakes.

More importantly, it will help you recognize and correct them promptly.

Let me ask again: Can you coach kids? Of course you can. What you choose to teach them, how much you teach them, how much fun they have, how much they like the sport, how happy the parents are, and how much your team wins may all be different issues.

Chapter 5

Clear and Simple – Assume Nothing

As an assistant coach for a kids' basketball team, I was telling the kids to rebound under both baskets – to fight harder for rebounds. One kid, listening intently, asked, "Coach, what's a rebound?" He wasn't the only kid who didn't understand. Now ask yourself what will happen when the coach, not having defined and demonstrated a rebound, goes on to explain that defensive rebounds must be cleared to the outside for a fast break in transition? Instructions need to be simple, clear, and demonstrated, demonstrated, demonstrated, and then practiced, practiced, practiced.

When coaching tee ball, I spent a lot of practice time teaching the kids about batting, catching ground balls, and throwing to first. When the first game rolled around, one of my boys got wood on the ball – his first in a game. We hollered, "RUN, RUN, RUN"! He did run – directly to third base. I had neglected to cover base running. What do they say about how to spell assume?

As a hockey coach, I told my players to keep their sticks on the ice. This is for safety, and because that is where the puck is. Also, it's the best position for reaction to most any situation. As we talked, one kid held his stick waist high. I looked at him and said, "Stick on the ice!" He looked around and did nothing. I pointed at him and said, more loudly, "Stick on the ice!" He finally dropped his stick on the ice. After an embarrassing moment, I showed all of them that the best position for almost all situations is to keep the blade of the stick on the ice, while keeping one's knees bent and head up. Demonstrate to the kids, with an action, what you mean and what you want them to learn.

The worst example of this was a football coach I saw screaming to his kids during a game to "PLAY FOOTBALL!" The veins stood out on his neck. He screamed it many times. "PLAY FOOTBALL!" It was certainly simple enough but not very clear. They thought that's what they were doing.

This is like hollering my dog's name at my dog. "BLUE! BLUE! BLUE!" The dog glances at me and says to himself, "Yep, that's my name. Do you want me to sit, stay, come, lie down, fetch, or what?"

When the coach hollers "play football," what happens? The kids who were doing something right probably decide that they were doing it wrong. Those doing something wrong still don't know it and will continue doing it wrong. The direction to "play football" doesn't help any of them. If all the coach can think of is gross generalizations like "play football," he or she should keep their mouth shut. Abraham Lincoln said, "Better to keep my mouth shut and be thought a fool, than to open it and remove all doubt."

Maybe you have some time or schedule limitations and want a partner to co-coach. I co-coached a girls' softball team and a boys' coach-pitch baseball team (where a coach pitched underhand to his/her own team). The other coach and I were very successful. This can work, but you have to put a little extra attention into coordinating the job, and the co-coach should also be a parent of one of kids on the team.

Co-coaching a boys baseball team, I remember telling the kids to put their glove on their knee when in the defensive-ready position. Jerry the co-coach had already told them not to put their glove on their knee but to have it ready by the knee. We had them fully confused! Before the pitch, we'd call to them to "be ready, guys." They would go through something that looked like a dance while glancing back and forth between us. We had both missed the point. While either method is OK, neither of us had explicitly demonstrated the important points: keep your feet apart, knees bent,

C'mon— — — Play
Football!!!

glove on or near your knee, and watch the ball/batter, not us.

We got together to agree on what “be ready” meant and had good success. We also worked with the kids to determine where the play was for every situation and kept it simple. Then, before each new batter, we would ask, “Where is your play?” Baseball moves “slowly” enough to allow you to do that, providing you have covered each situation in practice.

Co-coaching does have definite advantages. If something goes wrong, you can always blame the other guy. If a kid isn’t called about a practice or a schedule change, you can always blame the other guy. Also, if you are coaching alone, the team tends to take on your personality. You may be surprised by what you see. You might not even like what you see. One year, by about the second game, I looked around and saw my kids constantly telling each other what they were doing wrong. They were great critics. Listening carefully, I heard my own words coming from their mouths. If I had a co-coach I would have blamed him or her.

In general, you should coach the team alone. Don't share the responsibility and run the risk of confusing the kids and the parents. This doesn't mean that you have to do it all alone. It doesn't mean that you won't have a couple of assistant coaches. It does mean that the buck stops with one person – the coach.

Remember the golden rule of coaching kids during a game: One encouragement is better than three critiques. Even in practice, the best method is to demonstrate or have a kid demonstrate the correct way, rather than point out the one kid is doing it wrong.

As Gary Mack wrote in Mind Gym, "Many Little League parents don't realize the damage they do to their child's self-esteem with their negative comments. When you tell a Little Leaguer that he failed, you are telling him that he is a failure. Children internalize failure." He was referring to parents, but the same goes for coaches. Fear, harsh critiques, and embarrassment can work when kids get older, but not at young ages.

Think about your coaches when you were growing up. What did they do that you liked, what was most fun, and what kept you thinking about the important aspects of the game?

Do read a book about coaching your sport. Try to find a book that is directed at kids. Failing that, find a book that is structured so that the basics are separated from the advanced techniques. Look for the basic drills and plays. Weave them into your plan.

Some books are structured from the basics up. Absorb the basics and understand the skills progression that is age-appropriate for your group.

Must the coach have played the sport? Preferably yes, but you don't have to have played at the semi-pro level to coach kids. If the league needs coaches, go for it regardless of your experience. Coaches with no playing experience have been very successful. You may do a better job than someone with more credentials.

The parents and kids don't expect a professional performance from the coach. Kids expect you to make it fun for them. Parents expect you to teach the kids some basics in keeping with their age and prior experience. If the kids are going to have fun, the most significant thing you can do is avoid boredom. You need to find ways to make practices move quickly, be intense, and be fun. And you must involve the parents. You must find a way to relate to them and have them relate to both kids and parents.

One of my son's coaches purposely demonstrated the wrong way to do a task. He would laugh at himself, and the kids would laugh and go do it the right way. If they made a mistake on that task in practice he would say, "You did that as bad as I do!"

I used that general idea when teaching handicapped kids to ski. When they fell, I'd try to fall as quickly as possible, laughing all the way. They would look at me and laugh too. Then I'd tell them, "If you aren't falling, you aren't learning." I learned to ski backwards so the kids could follow me and still see what I was doing, and I learned to fall from that posture pretty well.

This is not to say that you shouldn't have behavior rules and enforce them, especially regarding rules about the handling of sticks and bats. Have a few well-thought-out rules. For example, a coach must expect quiet when he or she is talking. Thus, my number one rule: "When it's my turn to talk, it's your turn to listen." And if the kids aren't looking at you, chances are good they aren't listening.

Chapter 6

Behavior

Need I even say that an unwritten rule prohibits smoking, drinking, or swearing with the kids around! Some folks think that swearing makes their message more intense. This could be true with some adults, but it certainly isn't true with kids. Kids will only focus on the words, not the message. Intensity doesn't come from swearing. It comes from your practice time. And the kids will reflect your behavior – good or bad. I will discuss more on intense practices later.

I recently attended a family member's soccer game. The kids on the opposition were swearing on the field – foul stuff. The swearing was directed at the opposition players. When the coach was called on it, he had an attitude that was indicative of a problem. He shrugged and raised his hands – palms up – several times, meaning, "What can I do?" He also said it out loud.

But the answer to his question is simple. This coach only needed to say that he would talk to his team to tell them that swearing is not tolerated. If you don't understand how simple this is, shrug and raise your hands palms up! If you just did that, close this book and don't coach.

When it comes to officials making perceived mistakes, let the officials know you disagree but don't make much of it at the time. If you do, you could be giving your kids an excuse for losing. They can quickly decide that if the coach thinks the officiating is biased, they might not have a chance to win.

Only a tiny fraction of games are so close that an official's calls will affect the result. If you are loud and overbearing about it, the official may look closer than ever to find your team's transgressions. That's just human nature. Bite your tongue! Take consistent bias or serious complaints to the association and the other complaints to the reading room.

When coaching these young kids, you are typically coaching your own kid(s), too. Coaching your own kids, especially boys, is difficult. Kids may not take coaching from Mom or Dad well. Also, we coaches may not be as patient with our own children as we are with others.

What should you do? Put them on a different team? That doubles the number of trips and hours involved. Yet I heard this seriously suggested on a radio show once. No, just sit down with your assistants and make a deal. No coach will tell his own kid what to do or not do or how to do it. Instead, each coach will privately ask one of the other coaches on the team to tell their kid what to do.

Your kid will listen much better to the other coach. In fact, after practice your kid is likely to tell you exactly what the other coach said, as if you didn't know. Just say, "Oh yeah, that sounds like a good idea to me!"

You and your assistants need to display the kind of behavior that will inspire the kids, not distract them.

Chapter 7

The Organized Coach

Sandlot games have gone the way of the stay-at-home parent. Since organized kids sports seem to be the only practical alternative, the coach and league organizers must get organized. Let's do it in a way that is best for the kids.

There are two different levels of organization issues in kids' sports – league organization issues and coaching organization issues. League organization issues include planning issues such as how to divide the kids, what facilities will be used, who will coach, what rules will be used, and the schedule for practices and games. These are issues for the parent association or the government entity. Executing the plan is the coach's job.

Which responsibilities belong to the coaches and which to the association? The association should make the division of responsibilities very clear. We will get to that later. For now, let's stick to discussing the coach.

How do you get organized for effective coaching? First, you should attend the pre-season coaches meeting. You will get a roster, a place to practice and a game schedule, or at least learn when they will be available. This is a good time to ask a lot of questions about organizing and other subjects that will be covered later. Attend any coaching clinics available. And, of course, devour this book and at least one on your particular sport that is applicable to kids.

At your first team practice, find out as best you can which kid best belongs/fits at each position. This sometimes takes more time than you might want to spend, but it pays off in the long run.

Our son was chosen for an all star baseball team in the post season. His coach spent 90 minutes, the entire first practice, experimenting with every kid at third base. At the same time, he experimented with all the kids at first base. He hit the ball to third, watched the fielding, the throw to first, and the catch at first. He hit the ball to third, then he watched the fielding and the throw to first over and over again. The rest of the kids were running bases. He tried each kid only at those two positions.

It seemed like a very slow start. It was, however, the most well-spent practice of all. At that age, kids tended to pull the ball down third. The kid he chose for third was little for his age, but he was like a vacuum and had a great arm. The kid he put at first had an inaccurate throw, but he was big and could catch most anything thrown his way. The coach thus filled the two most important positions and, with a few more trials, learned enough about all the kids to fill the other positions.

In the in-house league, you may not have as much time to properly position kids. Also, the league may well have rules about rotating kids in various positions. At very young ages, it may be desirable to have such rotation rules. However, if you don't have those rules, rotation should be used as a motivator and to keep the kids interested, being careful not to overdo it.

It doesn't hurt to ask the kids where they want to play, providing you preface that by saying, "I may not play anybody where they want to."

Be especially cautious with your own kid. If you put him at quarterback without trying anyone else at that position you will rightfully open yourself up for criticism. You have an important balancing act to perform.

Experiment with kids at different positions. If they don't have confidence in your choices, something will be lacking. If they feel they had a chance, they will perform better wherever you put them.

Think about the key skills needed at key positions and assign the positions accordingly – like that baseball coach with first and third. Then watch the progress and don't be stubborn about changing positions

Your next big task: You need to fully understand the league rules. Know about how and when to substitute correctly, timeouts, fouls/infractions, and what is/isn't allowed. Put bluntly, you need to be able to "take advantage" of every rule.

My first year in girls softball, we knew that stealing bases was allowed after the ball had crossed the plate. We worked on steals to second, third, and home. We were the only team that worked on this. Therefore, we had a considerable advantage. The other coaches were so upset with us (they should have been upset with themselves) that the next year they got the league to eliminate base-stealing. We still won, but I digress.

Set goals for the season. Set one goal to "have fun," another to take the kids to a new learning level, and also set a win-loss goal. Don't be too aggressive with the win-loss goal, especially if you are a new coach. Evaluate how the talent was distributed among the teams and take that into account. Goals should probably be kept among the coaches and assistants.

In short, you can blunder along or get organized. Life will be much easier during the season if you get organized. Think about where the kids are now and where you want them to be at the end of the season. Figure out how many practices you will have during that interval. Write down what you want to cover at each practice, perhaps introducing a new concept at each practice while continuing drills from past lessons.

Chapter 8

Involve The Parents

You can't do a very good job of handling kids in intense practices by yourself. Even if you try, it isn't much fun. Get the parents involved. Make it clear when you volunteer that you are going to reserve the right to veto any kid because his parents won't get involved. If the parent doesn't help, the kid is out.

Square that with the association. You will see later that even the single parent with two jobs can help. Even a small responsibility for each parent will pay huge dividends for you, the team, and the parents.

Have your first team meeting with the kids and make sure at least one parent of each kid is present. Outline the league rules and your own rules. One of your rules should be that at least one parent from each family must be involved in the team.

Getting the parents involved will mitigate most of the finger-pointing and the frustration that goes with coaching kids. When a parent is involved, it becomes "their team," not "your team." This is called "taking ownership." They will look at you differently, and you will look at them differently.

It took me a few kid-seasons to recognize this fact, and it is a fact. For those of you who don't believe in facts, who believe that everything is just a matter of feeling, close this book and go jump into the nearest feel-good activity you can find. You'll be happier.

An example of the total lack of involvement is the soccer coach who asked his players' parents to be on the other side of the field from the team. The parents were not only uninvolved but separated by a playing field.

That coach probably didn't want to hear what the parents had to say. Yet the parents had plenty to say – about the coach. Listening to them, I can't say I blamed the coach for the total separation. But it was a bad decision not to involve the parents from the beginning.

Even if your season has started, recognize the wisdom here and change your attitude about the parents.

I heard recently about a college baseball coach who said he would accept only one phone call from a parent of his players per season, unless there was a family emergency. He told them so in a letter he sent home and when parents called the first time. He obviously wanted the parents to stay out of his process.

This may be an OK approach at the college level, but it certainly isn't practical at the primary level. In fact, it is self-defeating, arrogant, ill-advised, and simply wrong to exclude the parents of very young players.

The fact that it happens regularly doesn't make it the best approach. The parents will be regularly critical of the coach and the coach will be regularly critical of the parents.

Now you see the wisdom of getting the parents involved. But what can they do? If you have 15 kids on a team, that's a lot of parents. One parent involved for each kid makes 15 parents according to the old math. Here is the best method to productively involve them all:

Coach

You are coaching your own kid, so that is one guaranteed parent involved.

Assistant Coaches

Call for two assistant coaches. Outline the job as you see it. Assistants are expected to be at all practices and games. Since emergencies do arise, this will assure that two of the three coaches are at every game and practice. Folks with experience playing the sport are preferable, but experience is not required. Don't hesitate to take assistants who are eager as opposed to experienced. You will need to figure out how to make their time productive. I'll explain more on that later.

Bench Coach

This is someone who is dedicated to keeping order on the bench. He must be at all games and scrimmages or arrange for a substitute from among the parents. This is for your sanity and for safety's sake. It is especially necessary in games with bats, sticks, or helmets. You would appreciate the need for this person if you had seen the kid who was hit with a bat at my grandson's baseball game. This assistant keeps the kids controlled, in substitution order, and safe. Also he or she keeps positive chatter going on the bench.

Scorekeeper

This person keeps the scorebook and tracks the playing time, warns you when a player hasn't been in the game for the required or committed amount of time, executes substitutions on a prearranged schedule, and monitors the opposition to ensure that they also follow the playing-time rules. You will need to review with the scorekeeper the stats you wish kept. Make a "stat sheet" if necessary.

Equipment Manager

This is someone who picks up all the equipment and brings it to the next practice or game and ensures that all equipment is accounted for and gets in and out of your vehicle. You will have a lot going on before and after practices and games. Keep your time free for the kids and parents.

Telephone Team Manager

"Don't call me (the coach); we will call you." That's your mantra. If the weather looks poor, "Don't call me; we will call you." The coach makes one phone call for a schedule change, practice change, or any other change to the telephone team manager. The telephone manager divides the roster among the telephone team. The leader can also send an email, but don't rely on emails alone, as some folks won't see the email until it's too late. Also, the telephone is more personal and covers those without email. This will not preclude a parent from calling the coach for any other serious concern.

Telephone Team

Three or four parents are needed here. The roster is divided among them. The telephone team manager calls each one and tells them about the change. They, in turn, call their portion of the kids on the roster – about four calls each. This is a great way to involve the single parent who may already have two jobs.

Treat Leader

This person assures that a treat is there after each game. Nothing fancy is necessary – put a dollar limit on it if you wish. Less is more, especially if you're near meal time. The treat leader sets up a different parent for each game and/or practice. This leader makes sure that all parents participate. If you have 15 kids and only seven or eight games, then the treat leader will assign two parents for each game.

Parent-Couple

This couple makes sure that every kid is picked up from all practices and games. They will be the last to leave. They will commit to calling the parents of any kid left behind to ensure the kid and parents make contact. They also protect the kids from predators and the coach from false allegations.

Publicity Guru

The publicity guru should try to get the team name and kids' names into the local paper or on the radio. Or he and she simply make up a team newsletter for distribution on occasion, or at least once at the end of the year. This is a real keepsake, at least for this coach. The publicity guru also organizes the end-of-year party if you wish to have one. If you have involved the parents as discussed here, the party will be memorable regardless of the record.

This is not coaching by committee. You and your assistants are the only coaches. You will still make all the critical decisions, but you will get lots of friendly input and support from the parents.

Do not fall into the trap of thinking that "times are different now and this old method won't work." Some things never change, and most parents' attitude toward their kid is and will ever be unchanged. They will be pleased to be involved.

If they won't be involved, they are looking for a baby-sitting service and should be banned from the team and the league. Yes, some single parents with two jobs may need a break. But can't they make three or four phone calls on occasion?

Must all help come only from the parents? No, especially if there is a special older kid who will help. A middle school or high school kid can make a marvelous assistant coach. A coach with limited experience should look for such a young person to demonstrate and help. Such a person can serve as a great role model for your kids. One older brother or sister might volunteer instead of a parent. An older sibling or a neighborhood kid could be the head coach, providing they properly involve the parents. This would be difficult but doable.

COACH
Put a smile on their faces.
Invite them over to join you!

Chapter 9

Parent-Player Meeting

One important event to start parent involvement is an early team/parent meeting. Call one before the first practice, and preferably right after the coaches meeting. This will be a team meeting including all the kids. But also require at least one parent of each child to attend. Personally telephone each family. Make it clear that this is a requirement. If one parent isn't there, the kid doesn't play on your team. Make sure you don't make an exception for any player, especially not the star player.

Make a roster before the parent-kid meeting. Make sure to give a copy to each family. A copy of league rules should be made for each assistant coach. Write down and copy your rules for each family. Hand these out at the meeting, along with a copy of the game schedule and your practice schedule. Don't rely on every family having a computer or using it. Go with a hard copy. It eliminates excuses.

At the meeting, read your list of jobs aloud. Ask for questions. Discuss each job as necessary. Then ask for volunteers. You may have to say that the meeting isn't going forward until you have one parent from each family helping. Say again that you aren't going to do it alone. Outline the jobs no one has volunteered for and wait. Sometimes there will be a long pause before parents start to volunteer. Don't give them any choice.

Make sure you are prepared, and keep the meeting short. I've seen the most meaningless bunch of drivel put out at such meetings.

One year, our daughter signed up for a competitive hockey team. The parent-kid meeting was a disaster. It lasted over two hours. Nothing was written down or handed out. Except for that meeting, there was no parent involvement. The coaches were two good old boys who could barely skate, had never coached, and didn't ask for help.

There was a lot of talk about how expensive ice time is (a fact), but no talk about minimum playing-time rules. It turned out there weren't any. The team carried too many players. My daughter was quite capable and got good playing time. But many parents became unhappy when their children got little or no playing time.

Eventually, it became clear that one of the coaches' daughters was the superstar and phantom coach. Practices were a farce. Our daughter didn't learn one new thing all season. It seemed the team was purposely set up to get money from parents whose daughters weren't going to play in order to pay for ice time and tournament fees.

How did things end up? The team had some very good talent besides the superstar. They won the Minnesota State Championship for their age group. It was proof that talent can substitute for coaching.

It proved that coaches need not have played the game. And it proved that playing-time rules and parental involvement can prevent a lot of bitterness in the end.

You must make it clear to the parents that you have a life too. You are not a taxi service. If parents want to organize a plan, they can do so on their own. If they have doubts about practice because of the weather, they should just show up, unless they get a call from the telephone committee.

Make it clear to the kids and parents that you recognize that the art of coaching is not an exact science. You will make mistakes. Make clear that if parents wish to make suggestions or complain, they must do so in private, one-on-one with the coach, calmly and quietly.

You should reserve the right to decide whether a child continues to play for the team based upon the parents' cooperation and behavior. The message is: Behave as a parent should, or you and your kid will not be on our team. The association must back you in this.

When it comes to playing time, which a very important issue to most parents, you can give an evasive answer much like the kind that politicians give to tough questions. Or you can use good logic to tell them you will make every effort to make sure you meet and exceed league rules about playing time and that you will have help from the scorer/ timekeeper to assure the same.

If a team consists of kids of a couple of ages, say seven and eight-year-olds, let the parents and kids know that the older kids will usually get longer playing time. Next year, the younger kids will be the "old folks." Also tell the "old folks" that merely being older doesn't guarantee more playing time. They will need to hustle to get it. The better their cooperation, participation, practice attendance, and attitude, the more playing time they will get. Within the league rules about playing time your policy should be expressed as "more hustle, more time." This is the most powerful motivator the coach has. Use it wisely.

If the league doesn't have rules about playing time, then it is poorly organized. Lots of coaches and parents will waste a lot of time becoming wrapped up in this quandary. More on this later.

In the meantime, think through the issue and devise a meaningful and fair personal rule. Do some calculating: total minutes, innings, periods; total number of kid-minutes, innings, periods; number of games to be played, etc. Then determine a reasonable minimum time to commit to, realizing that you want to win, but not at all costs.

Chapter 10

Win At All Cost

At young ages, the primary difference between the win-at-all-costs coach and other coaches is in the treatment of the kids on the bottom of the totem pole. The "win-at-all-costs" coaches can be spotted because they find a way to drive off the bottom performers. They may have more difficulty doing this if the league has minimum playing-time rules. Without such rules, these coaches will just give the bottom performers token playing time or none at all.

The poorest performers may be singled out. They may be ridiculed in front of the rest of the team. When game or practice schedule changes occur, they don't get the word. During scrimmages, they almost always sit down at the start. They never start a game.

Everyone on the team is called by their first name except them. They are never asked to demonstrate a technique. I'm sure I've left out some of the "better" methods. When I was coaching, I used to ask other coaches why they didn't have the same number of kids I had. The answer was often that a couple of kids quit because "they really didn't want to play this sport." Sure, and a beer gut doesn't come from drinking beer!

Many of us revere Green Bay Packer coach and multiple Super Bowl winner Vince Lombardi, who said, "Winning isn't everything – it's the only thing!" I agree, as long as we are talking about pro sports. But this ain't about pro sports, it's about kids sports.

Bill Koch, a U.S. Cross Country champion and Olympic medal winner said, "Winning isn't everything in sports, striving for excellence is!" It was the venerable sports writer Grantland Rice who so wisely wrote:

For when the one Great Scorer comes,
To write against your name,
He marks not that you won or lost,
But how you played the game.

Let the parents and kids know you like to win. You will not apologize for a win. You will be proud to win. You wouldn't even mind winning every game. But it will not be a season of winning at all costs.

You will also, reluctantly, teach them to lose graciously. The other team played very well. On this day, they were the better team. If you say about the opponents that just beat you, then it is easier to take that loss. Describe those things the opposition did well. Relate that to some of the things your team did well. We can still be proud. We can still have fun. We will get them next time. Note a thing or two that you will work on in the next practice.

Don't ever blame the officials for a loss in front of your kids. Bad calls seldom make a difference in winning or losing. If you think there is a problem with a particular game or official, take it to the organization leadership.

All too often, one team has been "stacked" by the chief organizer, who also coaches. Their team just happens to get more talent – by accident, of course. Sure, and my hair loss is temporary.

If you get into a season before realizing this was done, tough it out and insist that the method of choosing teams must change next season. In this circumstance, I would not hesitate to tell the parents what has happened/is happening.

Have your scorekeeper keep a playing-time record for your own team and perhaps the opposition. It can be used to show a disgruntled parent. If you suspect that another coach is not following the playing-time rules, bring it to the league officials to find out whether they will monitor that team. If you see that team again in the schedule, have your scorekeeper or timer track their playing time as well as your own. Take the opposing coach aside with your timekeeper and explain what you see happening. If necessary, take the results to league officials.

Chapter 11

Protect the Kids and Yourself

Much has been said and written about the rare abuse of kids who are participating in sports. Most "solutions" favor some form of "screening."

I've read that some leagues require sex offender background checks for every manager, coach, and volunteer who routinely deals with players.

Now there is a decision from a bunch of folks who have never gotten slivers on a bench. What's the effect? It will discourage volunteers. We want all the parents involved, but we must first put them all through background checks? It will be very costly. Who wants to go through the hassle? It will have exactly the wrong effect. It will discourage parental involvement.

I once listened to a radio talk show where folks were talking about how to prevent perverts from getting at kids via coaching. "Require coaches to be screened by the city cops." "Access the state crime database." "Require psychological testing." "Call in the FBI." Callers went on and on about elaborate methods of identifying pedophiles. It was obvious that the discussion assumed that the coach was alone in the job.

How about false accusations? How can we prevent a coach from being falsely accused of abusing kids in any fashion? Can "screening" prevent that?

The simple, direct, and low-cost approach is to get the parents involved. Parent involvement alone will discourage the twisted ones. The "parent-couple" concept is built-in protection for the kids and for the coach. This couple must attend as a couple all practices and games. They are the last to leave. The coach should probably stay with them. They assure that each kid has been picked up by a parent. The league should require this. The coach should require this even if the league doesn't. It's good self-protection. There's no need to complicate this. Get the parents involved.

Since the parent-couple approach may require a considerable amount of time, a rotation of the couple may be needed. Have one set of parents coordinate this. It is a lot better than forcing every parent through a background check of questionable benefit, since all potential predators aren't "registered"!

Having said all that, if the league runs all head coaches through the national pedophile database then it is good protection for everyone. But it's not enough by itself. Doing that for some or all parents is a form of insanity. Discouraging the parents from participating by any method, no matter how well-intended, is plain nonsense.

Chapter 12

Intensity

Back in the early 1950s, a great Russian coach by the name of Anatoli Tarasov took charge of Russia's national ice hockey team. Before he retired in 1972, he had four Olympic gold medals and 12 World Championships. Experts all over the world praised him the greatest coach the game had ever known.

Canadian and American hockey people often claimed that the key to Russian hockey success was the length of their season and the quantity of their training time. Tarasov responded that it was rather the "tempo and the intensity" of each practice. His theory was "train hard and briskly or don't train at all." U.S. Olympic Coach Herb Brooks used the same technique to coach the "Miracle on Ice" hockey team of the 1980 Winter Olympics.

Practices

Often in practice, the coach is a "nice guy" – casual, joking, and easy-going. Come game time, however, the coach sounds like he is in an outhouse that was tipped on its door. You need to find ways to get the kids "up" for practices and, sometimes, to settle them down for games.

When I started coaching, I expected to have leisurely practices knowing that the kids would “step it up” for games. I was wrong! Practices need to be intense. I’m talking here about the coach and the drills. At game time, you (the coach) need to be less intense. You should still remain energetic, but you should be less vocal than you are in practice. The coach needs to be, in word and action, at a high pitch in practice drills. Then, come game time, he should tone down his voice and actions. The kids know that a game is going on and that it means more than practices. Even young kid understand that. But practice is a question of habit.

The team will start to form habits at practices. It is a fact of nature that humans are largely creatures of habit. Help your players form good basic practice habits and do them intensely.

Kids have a short attention span, so don’t have long practices. One hour of high-tempo practice is worth three hours of the other kind. Practices, including scrimmages, should be no longer than 90 minutes.

Use available practice time wisely. Write down a plan before each practice or, better yet, make one for the entire practice season. You probably won't stick with it religiously, but it will give you guidance as time progresses.

Do your practice planning on paper by closing your eyes and visualizing each drill. Imagine where the kids, the coaches, and you will be.

Think about where the lines may form and devise a way to keep the lines short. Or plan for another drill to be inserted where the line will be. For example, if you are working on a "give and go" routine with a line for the "give" and another for the return pass, it makes for two potentially long lines. Have an assistant coach form an identical drill. The lines will be half as long and the kids will get twice as much practice.

Make them work fast – as near to game conditions as possible. Insert a coach or one of the kids into the drill as a defender. Have enough balls available to assure an intense pace.

Don't stop practicing when the game schedule starts. There is a reason for that old adage "practice makes perfect." Intensity (or tempo and concentration) at your practices will, to a great extent, determine your intensity in games. It's that "extra something" you hear coaches talk about. It is often responsible for the "momentum" you hear announcers talk about.

Ask for a kid to volunteer to show the others how a drill is done. Don't always pick the same kid. Spread the glory around. When a kid is picked to demonstrate, he or she rightly thinks, "The coach thinks I'm good." That is exactly how you want every kid on the team to feel.

Watch for places in your practice where the kids are standing around. Work out a drill for those times. Have an assistant coach run that drill. Never assume that the kids know the basics. High standards, high expectations, high humor, and high practice intensity will produce the best results.

Scrimmages

End your practice with a scrimmage. Have an assistant coach be the official. Follow the same rules in scrimmages that the league will follow during games. Explain what violation occurred after every whistle. Stop scrimmages for quick coaching pointers. Have the kids stop and freeze when the "official," or you, blows the whistle. This will allow you to give more meaningful tips. Do it quickly and move on.

Catch the kids doing something right and let them know about it – right then. Every time you catch the kids doing something right and praising it, you will reinforce that behavior.

During practices and scrimmages, highlight any good progress for every kid. Do not fabricate praise, but do recognize when a kid does something a little better than before. "Atta boy/ girl!" "Way to go, Bill!" "Yes, Bob, well done!" "That's great, Jenna!" This rule also applies to games.

If you don't have enough kids to form two teams for scrimmages, you, the assistants, siblings, and parents can join in, but they must be asked to play at the kids' skill level.

Finish the practice and scrimmage with a short talk. Keep it very short or you will lose their attention. Tell the kids what they need to work on. Ask them to close their eyes and imagine themselves doing a particular move or play. This point cannot be overemphasized.

Pick a universal problem or drill that needs improvement. Ask the kids to close their eyes and picture a particular circumstance with you. Describe it. For example, "OK, guys, you are passing the puck to a teammate. You've picked someone in the open. Just as quickly as you pass, you are off toward the goal. Now picture yourself as the guy who gets the pass. See yourself returning the pass to the teammate who is breaking toward the goal." Do it again. Ask them to work on that move or play at home in the basement, yard and in their minds – visualization does help.

Game Time

During games, there isn't much you can do except keep your cool and continue teaching. Your teaching should be generally directed at those on the bench or just coming to the bench. You should still display high intensity with your words and actions.

You can yell "good stuff" to the kids in the game, but give minimal instruction. The kids in the game may be too occupied to hear, let alone respond. If you have complicated instructions, a time-out is in order.

Try to have fun, and try to keep the kids' intensity up without losing your cool or letting them lose theirs. If a kid does "lose it," it is best to get them out of the game for a little while.

If you feel you are loosing it or the team is having a really bad day, recall this simple prayer:

God, grant me the serenity to accept the things I cannot change,
The courage to change the things I can,
And the wisdom to know the difference.

B
Teaching
Concentration...
pays off!
H Venezia

After the game, have a quick wrap up meeting. Have the treat coordinator hold the treats until you're finished summarizing the highlights and the areas for improvement. If you lost, praise the other team: "Today they were the better team, but next time you can be the better team."

Chapter 13

Problem Parents

You have heard the same complaints about kids sports that I have. Many coaches say that the kids aren't a problem, the parents are the problem. I got an email from a good friend that tells the story about that kind of parent:

At one point during the game, the coach called one of his 8-year-old baseball players aside and asked, "Do you understand what cooperation is, what a team is?" The little boy nodded in the affirmative. "Do you understand that what really matters is that we win or lose together as a team?" The little boy nodded yes. Coach continued, "I'm sure you know that when an out is called, you shouldn't argue, curse, attack the umpire or call him a lousy bleep. Do you understand all that?" Again the little boy nodded. The coach continued, "And when I take you out of the game so another boy gets a chance to play, it's bad sportsmanship to call your coach a rotten piece of bleep isn't it?" Again the little boy nodded. "Good," said the coach. "Now go over and explain that to your mother."

Obnoxious behavior from any parent is a rare but serious problem. Let the parents know at the team meeting that loud-mouthed criticism of an official, coach, or player can only hurt the team's chances.

Even having covered this, it sometimes isn't enough. Sometimes a one-on-one with a parent is in order. It's probably best to call them on the phone. If you want the other parents to know what you are doing, then ask the troublesome parent (in front of the other parents) to stay around for a minute after the game.

Another technique a fellow coach used was to give the ref a "heads-up" about a troublesome parent, saying some "special treatment" might be needed. Referees should have the authority to put the game on hold until the troublemaker leaves the area.

I had a very lousy parent one year. As you might suspect, his wife had come to the parent-kid meeting – not him. He was obnoxious to both the officials and to me. I could hear some of it from the bench, but the parents later told me details that I didn't hear. I tried to ignore it – a bad decision. It was very divisive for the team and the parents. I made the mistake of not telling him to take a hike. It was the only bad season of 26 kid-seasons of coaching.

On occasion, a parent will interfere or try to take over your job. A friend calls this type of parent a "helicopter parent" because they hover over you. Take this parent aside and have a short discussion on the matter. Tell them you will recommend them for coaching a team next year, but this year it will be done your way.

If parents refuse to be involved or are troublemakers, they and their child are off the team. You need to cover this critical point with the league leadership beforehand. As we will cover later, the league should have a method for purging troublemakers. Left unchecked, a rare parent will create one of those situations we read about in the papers. Don't let it get anywhere close to that – get rid of them.

Few parents are real troublemakers. Most just want to have some say in what is going on.

However, there are some coaches who often say that parents are always complaining – to them, behind their back, to other parents, and to the association. These are the parents who say things like: "Coach doesn't play my kid enough." "Coach is playing favorites." "Coach isn't teaching them much." "The schedule was changed and we didn't hear about it." You get the picture.

What's wrong here? When I question the coach, it usually becomes apparent that the coach is a one-man show, or at best has one assistant who may not even be a parent. The parents aren't involved. Parents will be super-frustrated and critical when they aren't involved. They have no ownership in

Hey Coach!!!
Let My Jimmy
PLAY!!

the team. They only have ownership in their kid. There's an easy solution – involve the parents.

Chapter 14

The League

So much for parents and coaches. Let's get to the association leadership – well-meaning folks who determine policies and settle issues that are critical to the kids' and the coaches' experience.

Much can go wrong at this level. Often, league organizers get wrapped up in the need to draft a charter for the league. A charter statement that points out how important and "feel good" sports should be.

A coaching friend told of the endless arguments over the "goal statement" for his league. Several people arguing for over an hour on two different occasions. What a waste of valuable time. Do we need a goal/charter statement for the organization? Sure, but go to the Internet, find a statement you like and adopt it. Then get on to the important stuff.

The league needs to have clear-cut policies about seven issues. In no particular order, the seven most important things league officials should do (in addition to getting good coaches) are:

- Devise a method to purge the troublemakers from a team and the league.
- Write a policy for balancing player playing time.
- Write a policy for balancing team talent.

- Manage kid "drop out."
- Determine whether the league is competitive and/or noncompetitive.
- Hold training for the coaches.
- Obtain facilities and set and publish the schedule early.

These and other policy/rules should be carefully considered and then written down and given to every coach. The coaches should be given enough copies for every family on their team and told to have a team meeting to hand them out.

The league shouldn't expect the coaches to make copies. When coaches are given enough copies for the parents they will more likely hand them out, whether or not they see the wisdom in having a team meeting.

Some leagues require a parent to sign the policy/ rules and return a document to the league to assure they have been disseminated. When I see this done, I wonder how the administrators assure that the parents read the rules. Instead, require coaches to hold a team meeting and review the rules with the parents.

The need for addressing the first issue – purging troublemakers – is obvious. Yet it's often ignored. Instead, the leagues rely on hope, as in "Let's hope we won't have this problem."

The next three issues are important for obtaining "parity" in the league – a condition wherein each team has a roughly equal opportunity to win or lose. Parity also optimizes the importance of the coach. An outstanding coach can still win more than "their share."

Competitive, noncompetitive or both is a very important decision for the league. The answer may require different rules – about playing time, for example –and those rules need some consideration, too. All rules and policies for both the competitive and noncompetitive aspects of the league should be drawn up before the season starts.

The training of coaches is very spotty by my experience. Many leagues do it well, others not at all. The same with facility selection and scheduling.

Of course, the league organizers may be volunteers, too, and their time, like the coaches', is limited. So this discussion will address the optimum while realizing it may not be met. Use of this book should help with the limited time issue.

Chapter 15

Purge the Troublemakers

Troublemakers are a problem in all team sports at all levels. It is sometimes seen by coaches and not reported to the league. It is sometimes seen by coaches and kids but not by any parents. It is sometimes so horrific that it ends up in the newspapers and on TV. Some of these events can be prevented.

In these cases, a parent or other family member or friend repeatedly acts like a WOFATP (Waste Of Food And Toilet Paper – pronounced wo-fa-T-P). The league needs to have a method, established ahead of time, to purge this troublemaker. He or she is typically the parent who also doesn't help out with the team. They just stand back and complain about the coaches, officials, or league.

During my coaching career, I never saw a really effective method of handling a troublemaker. It came down to the coach saying, "That guy and his kid are out of here, or I am." This is a poor position to put a coach in.

On a plane trip, I met a coach who told me of a fine method of handling the troublemaker. Here's what his league did:

- The league authorizes each coach to warn the troublemaker and requires the coach to do it privately. They also create a First Strike Card. It clearly states that if the problem happens again, the parent and player involved are off the team. Each coach receives a card or two each season.

- The coach gives the card to a troublemaker at his/her discretion. The coach must immediately tell the league when a card is given and explain why – preferably in writing.
- The league then furnishes the coach with a Second Strike Card with the troublemaker's name on it.
- If necessary, the coach gives the Second Strike Card to that troublemaker. It tells the parent that he/she and the player are no longer part of that team, but they may contact the league office to be given one last chance on another team.
- The coach must immediately notify the league. If the family wants to try another team, they can. If they choose to go to another team, the new team coach is given a Third Strike Card with the parent's name on it.

- If that parent acts up again, the new coach presents the Third Strike Card and a "You're out of here!" Again, the new coach immediately notifies the league.

Three strikes and you're out! I love it. Maybe a Three Strikes card system is also needed for coaches who have ignored this book, or for coaches who yell obscenities and let their players yell obscenities at the officials, players, other coaches, or worse. You bet your britches – three strikes and you're out. Perhaps coaches should only be allowed two strikes?

Purging rules should be spelled out in the handouts for the parents. The parent can see or call the league to state their case anytime. Sounds like a fine method to me. I think it can significantly limit the ugly events that happen all too often in kids sports.

If I had had that Three Strikes card system when I was coaching, I probably would have used it three times in 26 seasons.

Whether or not you use this particular method, there must be a way of getting rid of the troublemakers.

Every league, almost always, has one or two. If they are not checked, fights and other extreme events, including death, can result. Too often, ugly things happen because the league didn't have a working policy to purge the WOFATPs.

Leagues run by government entities have a harder time doing this tough stuff. How can a government recreation district tell a taxpayer that he can't participate? This is another reason why leagues should be controlled by the parents, not government.

Once again: Parents should coach the kids and organize the program while the government should furnish the field, rink, park, or court and pledge to stay out of the process. The parents lead, the kids follow, and the government gets out of the way.

Chapter 16

Balance the Playing Time

Balancing the playing time is critical. Any kids sports organization must give serious thought to the rules on this crucial subject. Use pertinent criteria such as defensive and or offensive plays; innings, periods, at bats; minutes of playing time; or combinations of these or other criteria.

If the teams are made up of two age groups, should the rule be the same for first-year and second-year kids? The kids who stick with the program for a second year will likely get more playing time in the second year just because they have matured and probably improved. Do we expect approximately equal time? Can the method be easily measured by the team scorekeeper? Consider how to monitor the results – honor system, turn-in timesheets, and having a league official attend random games. Also consider how you will you handle disputes between coaches.

Nothing can sour kids and parents more than the perception that they are being "cheated" on playing time. Establishment of minimum playing-time rules will go a long way toward keeping all parents and kids happy without destroying the competition. This is also a giant step toward "parity."

Whatever rules are developed should, in my opinion, be for both the regular season and for playoffs. Changing rules for the playoffs sends a poor message to coaches, players, and parents: During the regular season, we were interested in parity; now we are interested in winning at all costs.

Some say that "competitive leagues shouldn't have such rules." I disagree. At these young ages, even competitive leagues should guarantee a minimum amount of playing time, though the competitive league can have different playing-time rules than the general league.

After all, according to one study, less than one in 100 kids playing sports will play college sports. Less than four percent of college players ever play pro sports. So put playing time into perspective.

At these young ages, kids shouldn't be pushed into a particular sport or pushed to play entire games, or be made a pawn in the process. Many studies have proved that playing time at very young ages makes no difference in the players' ability to excel at older ages. I contend that how much fun young kids have is far more important to their progress than their playing time. If they learn to enjoy the game, they will have a much greater chance of excelling at it.

Balancing the playing time is the first step toward parity in the league.

You can achieve parity by balancing the talent and balancing the playing time. These drawings illustrate that. Maybe a third sketch can be added to the drawing – one that shows an adult coach keeping a kid (littler than the other kids) from falling off the balance beam.

Talent
(Smaller) Talent
OK— But 3 innings
are 3 innings!

Chapter 17

Balance the Talent

Balancing the talent among the teams in the league is critical. When all is said and done, this aspect of league organization is both the most important and the most difficult to achieve.

Often, the person who does the organizing is also a coach. He or she may feel that getting the pick of the talent is the reward for doing all the organizational work. It's no surprise then when they win more than their share of the games. I've witnessed cases where the league organizer won every game. It was obvious that the talent wasn't spread around.

So what method is fair? The "sandlot method" is the best method going for balancing the talent. It is a fair draft system.

One year, my neighbor Gene and I decided to co-coach a girls' softball team. Each team was to carry 15 girls. The league had carry-over teams that included players from the past season. The team had a maximum of eight "carry-overs." Tryouts were held for all the new girls. Apple Valley, Minnesota, was growing fast then, so there was a lot of new talent. Each girl was to hit, run the bases, catch and throw. A league organizer pitched to all of the girls for consistency.

At the tryouts, Gene and I sat on separate benches and separately rated and ranked all the new girls with a method we had worked out ahead of time, using a scale of 1 to 10. A draft was then held to fill each team with 15 girls. Since we were a brand new team, we were given eight draft picks to fill our team to the "base of eight." Thus, we and the other new team had the opportunity to pick the best 16 players – eight each – in turn. Then all teams joined the draft according to the number of carryovers each had.

The other coaches seemed more interested in drafting who their daughter wanted on the team or who lived in their neighborhood. They didn't use a ranking method. We therefore drafted not just eight but 13 of the most talented girls for our team. Since our own daughters were among the best in the league, we had a very powerful team. These two years were the only back-to-back undefeated seasons in my coaching career. We had lots of fun, but the other teams didn't seem to enjoy it as much as we did.

Is it OK to have such lopsided results? Was that the best thing for the girls on all of the teams? The other coaches were certainly unhappy with our dominance. What went wrong here? The talent was nowhere near balanced.

In my opinion, coaches should have their own kid(s) on their teams. After that, what do we do? Organize by neighborhood and hope that the talent is randomly distributed? If the neighborhoods have about the same player population, this might work. If schools are running the show, the talent will be distributed according to school size. If the schools in the league are about the same size, the talent will be fairly evenly distributed. If they aren't, the biggest school will probably dominate.

But what method is best for an association? I think it's the universal tryout method, much like we used on the sandlot. This method, with a tryout, ranking, and draft, goes something like this:

- All the players, new and old, are put through the same drill(s).
- Two or more league officers/ coaches grade every player, whether they are on an existing team or not. The same method is used by all.
- The ranking is summarized by one method – say a 1-to-10 score for

each drill – then totaled. If three drills are used along with the 1-to-10 method, a perfect score is 30.

- Coaches are given a list ranking all of the players.
- Then the draft is conducted according to the ranking of the players. That is, any team that doesn't already have a top-ranked player drafts one. Then the remaining top-ranked and number two-ranked players are drafted with all teams participating.
- Each coach might be given one "personal draft" to get their kid's best friend on the team. This is a difficult issue, as the best friends may be of significantly different rank. If this is done, attention to the rank might cause an adjustment in draft order.

The same method could be used with league officials assigning the players to teams based only on rank. Even then, coaches should coach their own kids.

Of course this takes considerable planning for a one-time event. Even with the associated problems (kids who can't make the tryout, deciding which coaches rank the players, etc.), this is a very good method. Some equitable method must be found because balancing the talent is the second giant step toward parity.

Chapter 18

Dropouts

When dealing with teams of very young players, dropouts need to be carefully monitored by the league.

The league needs to be very diligent in watching coaches who always have one or more kids drop out for no apparent reason. These coaches are probably the "win at all costs" type. Unfortunately, especially when the league has playing-time rules, it isn't beneath those few coaches to find ways to drive off the low-talent kids. There are more ways than liver pills.

Absolutely the worst example of this kind of coach was once covered in a Sports Illustrated article. The baseball coach of a group of eight and nine-year-olds told the parents about the playoff schedule but suggested that no one tell the parents about a handicapped kid on the team. League rules called for every kid to play three innings. When the kid showed up anyway, the coach offered to pay one of his kids $25 to hit the handicapped kid during warm-ups. When a shot to the groin didn't do the job, the coach told the pitcher to "go out there and hit him harder." The next shot in the face and ear properly put the coach in court. Turns out the coach was also facing charges for assaulting his fiancée.

Certainly this is an extreme case. But minor versions of this story happen all the time, even though once is too often.

Coaches should be required to report every dropout promptly. The league should ask why the player dropped out and then check out the answer. Someone in the organization needs to call the parents, question them, and talk to the player if the parents agree. Would the kid play for another coach? If so, a swap of equally ranked players would be in order.

The league should also talk to one or two other parents from the team, asking some piercing questions. Was the player who dropped out treated differently than others? If the coach seems to have "driven off" a low-skill player, league officials must talk to the coach and let him know, in no uncertain terms, that this is unacceptable. A First Strike Card for the coach is in order. The coach must understand that the league isn't going to tolerate such action. This won't have to be done often once word gets around.

Are children who move into the league during the season going to be put on a team? If so, they need to be ranked and placed on a team that had a dropout of the same rank.

The league should have a meaningful policy about dropouts, and it should be written and reviewed with the coaches before the season starts. This is the third step toward parity in the league.

Chapter 19

Competitive or Noncompetitive

The "competitive vs. noncompetitive" issue is the hottest issue in kids sports. What does it mean to be noncompetitive? Does it mean that we just don't keep score, or is there more to it? Do we tell the kids to just have fun and get along? The approach isn't very realistic – especially in football or hockey!

An absence of scorekeeping works well until about age seven. In tee ball for five and six-year-olds, the noncompetitive rules work OK. For example, everybody bats every inning, and the last person up gets a base-clearing hit, whether or not the hit gets out of the infield. The batting rotation is such that every kid gets a turn to "clear the bases." Similar methods for other sports may work at that age. Although one wonders who is being fooled by the tactics, the kids or the parents?

Beyond that age, however, what can be done? You either have to drastically change the rules or live with the competition of sports and the natural competitiveness of kids. Face it, life is competitive. Life isn't fair, either. Still, league officials should constantly strive to make the league as fair as possible.

Many leagues use the "Traveling Team" or "Competitive Team" approach. This assumes there are enough kids in the league to make at least one traveling team. The best kids in the league are offered a chance to compete with the best from other leagues. Voluntary tryouts are usually used to sort out the best kids for the competitive team(s).

Often, traveling teams are set up without any intention of balancing playing time. I think even traveling teams should have rules that balance playing time. Again, not necessarily equal time, but a minimum playing-time rule. Imagine how parents feel if their kids are selected for an all-star team and don't play, or played only a token amount.

The traveling league should seek parity by examining the number of kids each league has to draw from. If the more populated leagues are required to have more than one traveling team, the talent will be better balanced, more kids will be participating, and some parity will result.

Does this mean that the kids in the rest of the league are noncompetitive? We could call them that if it makes some folks feel better, but who are we kidding? "Noncompetitive" in sports is an oxymoron. It is a wish masquerading as a policy!

Denying competitiveness among Americans is like walking to a lakeshore and denying the urge to skip a rock. "Traveling" and "in-house" are more meaningful terms.

Chapter 20

Plan and Communicate

Needless to say, league officials must obtain facilities for games, and sometimes for practices. This is a difficult process I've never been part of. Leagues typically do a very good job with it.

Most leagues also do a pretty fair job of publishing the season schedule. The schedule should be handed to all parents via the coach.

It's also an excellent idea to occasionally print a newsletter. The best-organized league I witnessed was the Apple Valley, Minnesota, kids hockey. The following newsletter came out in April:

Next Season Notes:

- *Registration will be in September – time and dates to be announced.*
- *Education Week Clinics are planned for Oct. 19, 20, 21, and 22.*
- *Traveling Team tryouts are the week of Oct. 23, with team selection by Oct 29. Practices will start the next day.*
- *In-House tryouts are in mid-November, with teams selected by early December.*
- *Indoor practices will start in December.*
- *League play will start Christmas Week.*

- *The Big Apple Tournament will be Jan. 18, 19, 20, and 21.*

That is what you call planning ahead. Clinics were held for coaches and kids, and there were in-house tryouts for balancing the talent.

These folks were extremely well-organized, and the results showed. The kids who went through that program progressed up the learning curve with superior speed. The ultimate result was a Minnesota State High School Hockey Championship for Apple Valley High School. I was very proud to coach the kids at the younger ages who would eventually become part of that success.

Chapter 21

Coaches' Training

The league needs to address the high probability that coaches will require some training. There will most likely be new coaches every year. Some older coaches can also use some training. A few can probably teach the clinic. Pick one who is interested and qualified. Perhaps the high school coach would do the clinic. One person might do the drills and another cover the dos and don'ts of coaching.

Clinics should be held very early in the season, preferably before the team meeting and first practice.

The clinic need not be long. In fact, it's best kept to 60 or 90 minutes. The emphasis should be on drills and the dos and don'ts for both the drills and for coaching in general.

Clinics should be held on the field/court/rink. The clinic leader should draft some kids to aid in the drill demonstrations. If there are too many drills for the age group, a second clinic may be in order.

Diagrams of drills should be made, and each coach should get a copy to help him remember all of the drills.

Emphasis should be on demonstrating intensity in practice. The drills should thus be done with speed and intensity. Take time for discussion between drills. The clinic leader should encourage questions.

The leader or a league official should emphasize the importance of the requirement of parental involvement – again and again.

A book in the sport should be recommended. If the book is not tailored to the age group, the sections that are applicable to the age group should be noted. A copy of this book might be given to each coach by the league (a shameless marketing pitch).

It goes without saying: The better the clinics, the better the practices, the better the games, the better the competition, and the better the learning.

Chapter 22

Schools and Kids Sports

Organizing sports in schools is a natural. These days, though, some government schools seem to want to drop sports – and often physical education – altogether.

Amanda Spake wrote in US News & World Report, "Now only 8 percent of elementary schools and 5.8 percent of high schools offer daily PE in all grades." This is amazing but true. It's probably also why recreation districts have grown so fast. Could it also be a reason for high dropout rates? Maybe it's also the reason that so many kids' guts and butts have grown so much?

Many modern schools are so big that few students make the sports teams. The result is overweight and out-of-condition kids, many of them with too much pent-up energy. The situation doesn't match the wishes of a vast majority of parents, at least in my informal surveys. If a ball team carries 20 players, it represents 10 percent of a school of 200, but just 1 percent of a school of 2,000 students. In a small school, a half-dozen sports teams would involve over half of the school population. This is probably a good argument for reducing school size, but it is also a good argument for physical education in schools.

A few government schools even go so far as to try to prevent the neighborhood association or recreation district from using school facilities. Unforgivable!

Yet, schools are the perfect place to organize PE and sports for kids. Kids need a break from class time, and they need to work off some of that energy. Physical education should be mandatory for all kids. In lieu of physical education, after-hours intramural or school-team sports should be offered for those kids and parents who wish to participate. They are at school, why bus or drive them elsewhere to play? The facilities are right there – let's use them!

Schools that have organized sports should have a "no pass – no play" rule that covers every subject. I would readily endorse a requirement of a "C" grade or higher in all subjects for students who play sports. Let the kids know that schoolwork is more important than sports. Period. Kids who are competitive will want to participate in after-hours sports and may keep their grades up to do it.

Even when the school is organizing sports, parents should be expected to help out. Parents are much more likely to do what is best for the kids.

"Oh, but the parents don't have time," say some administrators and teachers. Last time I checked, there were lots of parents who would volunteer if they were asked. The common cop-out from some teachers, administrators, and unions is that "parents aren't involved." Have the parents been asked? Has anyone called them? Has the school sent a note home with the kids? Has anyone put an article in the local paper asking parents to volunteer?

The primary and middle schools once had enough money to offer physical education and intramural sports. What has happened? Do you remember voting to eliminate sports or physical education from schools?

Could it be that the administrators, school boards, and unions played the "Washington Monument Closing Game"? They say with an almost imperceptible whine, "We don't have enough money to do what needs to be done, so we will have to cut the sports, physical education, band, music or whatever program."

The tax-dollars-per-student figure has increased far faster than the rate of inflation. The students-per-classroom number is the same or lower than when I was in school. Some people don't like to address those facts.

"Well, our job is teaching, not sports," they say. Are there no lessons to be learned through sports? Can't students learn to "feel good" about themselves in sports as well as in the classroom? Won't involvement in sports make better students?

Sports are like any other extra-curricular activity. The more students take part in those activities, the more they and their parents feel that they "belong." And that feeling will invariably translate into better performance in core-subject learning.

One also needs to ask, is some of the violence seen in today's schools occurring because kids aren't physically challenged? An hour of physical activity for every kid, every school day is good for everyone involved. Intramural or inter-school sports are a proven way to get that activity.

See that "form"? –
Talk about your great
Coaching!"

Chapter 23

Recreation Districts and Kids Sports

Recreation Districts (read Government Tax Districts) have been created to fill the gap left by the schools and working parents. Generally, they do a very credible job. However, some rec districts tend to build an empire by offering something for everyone.

District offerings conducted with volunteer leadership – coaching, in our discussion – are the best approach in my opinion. If parents don't volunteer, then the activity simply shouldn't be offered. If parents don't care enough to volunteer in order to implement and maintain the activity, then the activity isn't needed. This is the "litmus test" of the worthiness of any recreational activity to be paid with tax dollars.

"But some of the parents are willing to pay a fee for their kids." So what? The course or sport is already funded primarily by taxes. Now some parents want to pay a fee to get out of helping. How generous! Parents who aren't willing to volunteer are, in my opinion, looking for the rest of us taxpayers to baby sit their kids.

Some government recreation districts have no incentive to apply such "make sense" rules. They, in fact, have incentive to grow their jobs as taxes and fees allow. They also have no incentive to involve the parents. They would prefer to hire "professional" coaches. I'm sorry, folks, but those are the facts.

This doesn't mean that the recreational district staffers are bad people. On the contrary, they are typically very caring and concerned folks. They like kids and do a very good job considering the circumstances they are in. Deep involvement of the parents, however, would mean an even better job.

Chapter 24

Rewards and Beginning

In short, you can and should coach kids, or help the coach or the organization. Do it. Go for it. You will get more out of it than you put in. The rewards are endless.

My coaching career has given me rewards throughout my life. I have a jacket that the kids (parents) bought me and presented at our year-end party. It is one of my most precious possessions. I also still have the thank-you notes, drawings, and poems from the kids on my teams. It is special when my own kids tell me they really appreciated my time with their teams. There aren't financial rewards, however. If I'd put the hours I spent coaching into earning and investing, I'd probably be considerably dollar-richer today.

I played men's and old-timers hockey until about age 55 and coached kids' hockey (boys and girls) many of those years. My kids watched, played on my teams, and later played with me.

I never realized what it meant to my kids until my youngest sent me an article from ESPN.com about kids watching their professional dads compete. My son wrote, "I thought the article was great. He [the author] only missed one point. He kept stressing how it was extra cool for these kids because their dads play in the NHL. I don't think it matters to young kids whether it's NHL or old-timers, it's just cool to see your dad competing and setting a positive example. Heck, that you played with my Jr. High gym teacher was just as impressive to me as if you'd played with Gordie Howe."

The primary reward for you will be in knowing that you have enriched the life of a kid and taught him or her something about a sport that you like. Your kids and the other kids you coach aren't very likely to become superstars or even continue to play the sport. But they are very likely to become a fan of the game, a better person, a better worker, a better boss, or even a better politician.

When they see you in later years and tell you that they really had fun playing for you, you'll know that you succeeded. One of my sons became a sportscaster and sports talk show host. He is well-known in the Green Bay, Wisconsin, area as the "Rookie." ESPN sometimes calls him for "insider" information. He probably wouldn't admit that the old man was an influence in his career choice, but some things just don't have to be spoken. He still plays and loves sports that I coached him in. My daughter has coached kids' soccer, and I see some of the old man's teaching coming through. My other son coaches his and other kids in a couple of sports.

It's rewarding enough to have a child you coached see you on the street or in the grocery store and smile and say, "Hi Coach!"

Can we combine the best of the sandlot with organized youth sports? Can some sandlot culture be used in competitive leagues? Can we combine the best of sandlot with competition? Can the kids, parents, and coaches on both sides feel like winners?

This book may not have answered all of those questions, but hopefully it has made you think about what is best for the children – not what is best for the parents, the teachers, the city, the coaches, the administrators, the school board, or the recreation district – but what is best for the kids. You are the right person to answer these questions.

So if you want to coach, help, or organize, do it! Go for it. It is very likely best for the kids.

Index

A

Abraham Lincoln *37*
Activity *21, 56, 139, 142*
Adult *19, 21, 24, 42, 45, 110*
Advantages *21, 40, 53*
Age *13, 18, 24, 26, 32, 41, 42, 47, 51, 52, 68, 69, 71, 84, 108, 109, 124, 129, 132, 133, 146*
America *17*
American Hockey *80*
  Americans *125*
Anatoli Tarasov *79*
Approach *14, 24, 27, 57, 58, 124, 142*
  Parent-Couple Approach *77*
Assistant *47, 48, 53, 59, 62, 84, 92*
  Paid Assistant *27*
Assistant Coach *(see Coach)*
Association *24, 28, 47, 50, 56, 69, 92, 95, 116, 136*
Attention *38, 81, 84, 117*
Attitude *46, 57, 62, 69*

B

Baby-sit *28, 62, 142*
Background Check *75, 76, 77*
Backyard *20*
Ball *11, 20, 36, 38, 51, 53, 82, 136*
  Ground Ball *32, 36*
Base Running *36, 51*
Basics *13, 32, 41, 42, 81, 83*
Basketball *13*
Behavior *43, 46, 48, 68, 84, 90*
Bill Koch *73*
Boys *8, 23, 36, 47, 67, 146*

C

Career *102, 115, 147*
Challenge *12, 19, 26, 80, 139*
Champion *73*
Championship *68, 79, 129*
Change *40, 60, 72*
Choice *20, 24, 28, 66, 147*
Choices *52*
Clinic *50, 128, 129, 131, 132, 133*
Coach *8, 9, 11, 12, 13, 14, 15, 18, 24, 26, 28, 29, 32, 33, 34, 36, 37, 40, 41, 42, 43, 46, 47, 50, 51, 56, 57, 58, 60, 62, 63, 67, 68, 69, 72, 73, 74, 76, 77, 80, 81, 82, 83, 90, 91, 92, 96, 97, 98, 99, 102, 103, 104, 108, 110, 115, 116, 117, 120, 121, 128, 129, 131, 132, 133, 142, 145, 146, 147, 148*
Coach (continued)
Assistant Coach *35, 40, 58-59, 63, 66, 82, 83*
  Baseball Coach *52, 59*

Bench Coach *59*
Co-coach *38, 40, 114*
Football Coach *37*
Head Coach *8*
High School Coach *132*
Hockey Coach *36*
Paid Coach *27, 29*
Professional Coach *26, 147*
Soccer Coach *56*
Win-at-all-costs coach *71*
Volunteer Coach *15, 26*
Youth Coach *13*
College Athlete *18, 19*
Communities *29*
Competition *14, 18, 22, 23, 24, 108, 124, 133, 148*
Competitive *11, 23, 24, 67, 97, 98, 123, 124, 125, 137*
Competitive League *(see League)*
Consequences *17, 18*
Contest *19*
Criticism *52, 90*
Critique *40, 41*
Culture *24, 148*

D

Decision *57, 62, 76, 91, 98*
Defensive *36, 38, 107*
Degree *26*
Demonstration *132*
Diagrams *132*
Direction *37*
Discussion *13, 76, 91, 99, 132, 142*
Doubt *33, 37, 68*
Dropouts *97, 110, 119, 120, 121, 136*

E

Effective *25, 50, 102*
Encouragement *50, 132*
ESPN *147*
ESPN.Com *146*
Excuses *66*
Expectations *33, 83*
Experience *12, 13, 21, 33, 42, 58, 63, 95, 98*

F

Failure *31, 32, 41*
Fee *67, 142*
Fight *20, 105*
Fitness *17*
Football *13, 20, 37, 124*
Frustration *20, 56*
Fun *17, 20, 25, 33, 34, 41, 42, 53, 55, 73, 83, 85, 109, 115, 123, 147*

G

Game *18, 23, 31, 32, 33, 36, 37, 40, 41, 46, 47, 50, 58, 59, 60, 61, 68, 70, 72, 73, 74, 77, 80, 81, 82, 83, 84, 85, 86, 90, 91, 108, 109, 114, 127, 133, 138, 147*
Baseball Games *59*

Football Games *20*
Gary Mack *41*
Girls *23, 38, 53, 114, 115, 146*
Goals *53, 85, 96*
Win-loss goal *53, 120*
Gordie Howe *146*
Government *26, 27, 28, 50, 105, 135, 136, 141, 142*
Gym *41, 146*

H

Habits *81*
Handicapped *43, 120*
Herb Brooks *80*
Hockey *13, 36, 80, 124, 128, 146*
Hoop *20*

I

Incentive *142*
Instructions *33, 36, 85*
Interest *26*
Intramural Sports *(see Sports)*
Involvement *56, 65, 67, 68, 76, 132, 138, 143*

K

Kids *11-15, 18, 19, 21, 24-26, 28, 31, 32-38, 40-56, 58-63, 65, 68, 69, 71-77, 80-85, 89, 95, 101, 104, 105, 108-110, 117, 119, 120, 123-125, 129, 132, 136-139, 142, 143, 145-148*

L

Leader *60, 132, 133*
Treat Leader *61*
Leadership *74, 92, 95, 142*
League *11, 13, 14, 33, 41, 42, 49, 50, 52, 53, 56, 62, 66, 69, 70, 72, 74, 75, 77, 83, 92, 96-99, 101-105, 108, 109, 113-117, 119-121, 124, 125, 127-129, 131, 133, 148*
Competitive League *109, 148*
League *(continued)*
Noncompetitive League *24, 97, 98, 25*
Learning *18, 19, 43, 53, 129, 133, 139*
Listening *35, 40, 43, 57*
Litmus test *142*

M

Manager *60, 76*
Equipment Manager *60*
Telephone Team Manager *60*
Mantra *27, 60*
Meeting *50, 56, 65, 66, 67, 80*
Parent-Player Meeting *65-67, 91*
Team Meeting *90, 97, 98, 132*
Mistakes *14, 15, 33, 34, 46*

N

NHL *146*
Noncompetitive *123-125*
Noncompetitive League *(see League)*

O

Old-timers *146*
Olympics *80*
Opportunity *18, 98, 115*
Organization *14, 15, 24, 27, 29, 50, 74, 96, 107, 113, 121, 145*
  Organizational Work *114*
Outcome *18, 26*

P

Parents *11, 12, 13, 19, 21, 24, 25, 26, 27, 28, 29, 34, 38, 40, 41, 42, 49, 50, 55, 56, 57, 58, 59, 60, 61, 62, 63, 65, 66, 67, 68, 69, 70, 73, 74, 76, 77, 84, 89, 90, 91, 92, 95, 97, 98, 101, 102, 103, 104, 105, 108, 120, 121, 124, 125, 128, 132, 133, 136, 137, 138, 139, 141, 142, 143, 146, 148*
  Helicopter Parent *91*
  Volunteer Parents *28*
Parity *98, 108, 109, 117, 125*
  League Parity *98, 109, 121*
Partner *38*
Performance *18, 42, 139*
Piggy-move-up *20*
Pitcher *120*
Playground *20*
Pledge *11, 26, 27*
Practical *18, 33, 49, 57*
Practice *29, 32, 33, 34, 36, 40, 42, 43, 46, 47, 50, 51, 54, 55, 58, 60, 61, 65, 67, 68, 69, 73, 77, 80, 81, 82, 83, 84, 127, 128, 132, 133*
  Team Practice *51*
Preparation *18, 20*
Priority *33*
Problems *12, 20, 27, 117*
Professional *26, 27, 146*
Progress *53, 84, 109*
Progression *42*
Publicity Guru *62*
Puck *20, 36, 85*

Q

Qualification *32*
Quarterback *52*
Questionable *77*
Questions *24, 46, 50, 66, 69, 81, 121, 132, 148*

R

Rebound *35, 36*
Recreation *11, 24, 26, 27, 29, 105, 136, 141, 142, 148*
  Recreational *142, 143*
Rewards *17, 18, 33, 114, 145, 146, 147*

Role Model *18, 19, 63*
Rookie *147*
Roster *50, 60, 61, 66*
Runner *17*

S

Sandlot Method *114*
Sandlots *14 19, 21, 24, 26, 48, 116, 148*
Schedule *72, 74*
  Game Schedule *50, 66, 82*
  Playoff Schedule *120*
  Season Schedule *128*
School *18, 20, 24, 27, 29, 116, 135, 136, 137, 138, 139, 141*
Elementary School *20, 136*
High School *13, 14, 63, 129, 136*
  Middle School *13, 32, 63, 138*
School board *148*
Score *24, 116, 123*
  Great Scorer *73*
  Scorer/timekeeper *69, 74*
Scorekeeper *59, 74, 108*
Scrimmage *59, 72, 81, 83, 84*
Season *15, 32, 50, 51, 53, 54, 56, 57, 67, 73, 74, 80, 82, 91, 98, 103, 104, 108, 114, 115, 121, 128, 132*
Separation *24, 57*
Soccer *13, 46, 147*
Softball *13, 53, 114*
Sports *11, 12, 13, 14, 15, 17, 18, 19, 21, 24, 25, 26, 28, 32, 34, 41, 42, 50, 58, 72, 73, 75, 96, 109, 124, 125, 133, 135, 136, 137, 138, 139, 142, 147*
Girls Sports *23*
  Intramural Sports, *138, 139*
  Kids Sports *17, 21, 26, 28, 49, 50, 72, 89, 96, 104, 107, 123*
  Team Sports *13, 18, 27, 101, 137*
  Youth Sports *24, 28, 148*
Sports Illustrated *120*
Sportsmanship *90*
Stage *13*
Strategy *31*
Strengths *20*
Success *38, 80, 129*
Super Bowl *72*

T

Talent *32, 53, 68, 74, 96, 109, 113, 114, 115, 116, 117, 120, 125, 129*
Talk *84*
Taxes *27, 28, 142*
Teacher *20, 24, 26, 33, 137, 146, 148*
Team *11, 15, 18, 21, 34, 38, 40, 46, 47, 53, 56, 58, 62, 65, 66, 67, 68, 69, 72, 73, 74, 81, 83, 84, 86, 90, 91, 92, 96, 97, 98, 102, 103, 108, 113, 114, 115, 116, 117, 119, 120, 121, 128, 136, 146*

Baseball Team *38, 51*
Basketball Team *35*
Carry-over Team *114*
Coach-pitch Baseball Team *38*
Competitive Team *124*
Hockey Team *67, 80*
Ice Hockey Team *79*
Softball Team *38*
Traveling Team *124, 125, 128*
Teamwork *18, 19*
Technique *41, 72, 80, 91*
Tee Ball *36, 124*
Telephone Committee *68*
Telephone Team *60*
Telephone Team Manager *(see Manager)*
Terry Frei *19*
Three Strikes *104*
First Strike *102-103*
Three Strikes *(continued)*
Second Strike *103*
Third Strike *103-104*
Time *28, 29, 46, 52, 59, 60, 69, 70, 74, 77, 96, 99, 102, 108, 114, 132, 137, 146*
Game Time *80, 81, 85*
Ice Time *67*
Playing Time *67, 68, 70, 72, 96, 98, 107, 108, 109, 120, 125*
Practice Time *36, 46, 51, 81*
Training Time *80*
Timeouts *53, 85*
Transition *36*
Trend *26*
Troublemakers *27, 91, 92, 96, 98, 101, 102, 103, 105*
Tryouts *114, 117, 125, 128, 129*
Tryout Method *116*

U

Umpire *19, 90*

V

Vince Lombardi *72*
Volunteers *24, 55, 66, 76, 99, 142*

W

Waste of Food and Toilet Paper (WOFATP) *102, 105*
Weakness *20*
Win *18, 23, 34, 46, 70, 73, 90, 98, 108, 114, 148*
Winners *12, 24, 148*
Winning *72, 73, 74, 83, 108*

Y

Yogi Berra *18*
Youth Sports *(see Sports)*